The Little Book Of Ketamine

Kit Kelly

Ronin Publishing
Berkeley, CA

www.roninpub.com

THE LITTLE BOOK OF KETAMINE
ISBN:978-0-914171-97-3
Library of Congress: 99-066708
Copyright © 1999 by Ronin Publishing, Inc.

Published by
RONIN PUBLISHING, INC.
PO Box 3436
Oakland CA 94609
www.roninpub.com

Printed by Data Reproductions Corporation
Distributed by Publishers Group West

Project Editor: Beverly Potter
Technical Advisor: Dr. Karl Jansen, MD, PhD
Cover Design: Judy July, Generic Type
Contributor: Dan Joy
Editor: Barry Katzman
Layout: Renee Richardson

First printing 1999

Acknowledgment

Researching and putting together *The Little Book of Ketamine* was the way it is "suppose to be" in the psychedelic community—helping one another for the greater good. Folks from Erowid, Lyceaum and *TRP (The Resonance Project: The Journal Of Modern Psychedelic Culture)* were generous with information and photos. Dr. Karl Jansen, the world's leading authority on the recreational use of ketamine, opened his research to us and provided helpful feedback on the manuscript. James Kent, publisher of *TRP*, provided a fascinating perspective on ketamine as a conundrum. We greatly appreciate their assistance.

Notice to Reader

Information presented in this book is made available under the First Amendment of the Constitution. It is a general overview of recreational use of ketamine and should not be considered medical advice. The publisher and author do not claim medical authority. As you will discover in this book, ketamine is a fascinating, but extremely dangerous drug. Should you contemplate using ketamine, consult your doctor or other qualified health practitioner first. Readers are cautioned that ketamine is legal when used medically, in a licensed facility, by a licensed medical doctor; it is illegal when used recreationally. Even simple possession of ketamine is a crime.

Table Of Contents

    Dr. Karl Jansen
    The Resonance Project
    The Vaults of Erowid
    The Lycaeum
    Books for Independent Minds

The Ketamine Konundrum

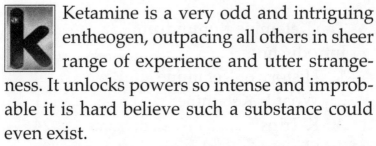Ketamine is a very odd and intriguing entheogen, outpacing all others in sheer range of experience and utter strangeness. It unlocks powers so intense and improbable it is hard believe such a substance could even exist.

At first glance it may look like a simple pet anesthetic, but when you actually try ketamine it seems to violate all boundaries of what we generally think is possible. While the notion of cosmic journeys in a cat tranquilizer may seem silly, ketamine is really much more complex than it appears. In fact, everything about ketamine is paradoxical, which is why I refer to its mere existence as a "Konundrum."

Konundrum I
Ketamine is synthetic.

It is unlikely enough that you would find a metaphysical wormhole in a simple fungus, cactus, or jungle shrub, but finding one in a little glass bottle manufactured by Parke Davis is just too weird for words. It is like finding psychic rocket fuel in your eardrops—intense. All other psychedelics are grown by Mother Nature herself or are carefully synthesized by craftspeople who have an immense passion for what they do. Ketamine, on the other hand, is stamped out on an assembly line and even comes with a little instruction booklet (often in many languages). If you do the right dose you get the desired effects. It's just that simple.

Konundrum II
Ketamine transcends time and space.

It is unusual enough that ketamine does a great job at keeping people safely unconscious during surgery, but the fact that it can also catalyze inner visualization, out-of-body experiences, near-death experiences, lucid dreaming, time distortions, trans-dimensional shifts, etc. is too bizarre to believe. I would not believe it myself if I hadn't had first-hand experience to prove it, but it is true. It can do all that stuff and more. It is the proverbial Philosopher's Stone, it has its own patent number, and it's illegal.

Konundrum III
Ketamine is addictive yet is used to treat addiction.

Unlike all other psychedelics that eventually say "No more," ketamine incessantly entices you to "do just a little more." The only problem is that there is no such thing as topping out on ketamine, there is only bottoming out, and the bottom is a long, long way down. You can take it for months, weeks, even years and it will never quit you. It will always continue to give and give and give just a little more—for a price, of course. The addictive demon has the power to cure as well, and has been used to treat chronic alcoholics with success. It can be a poison, a medicine, a drug, and much more. How it reacts depends largely on how you approach it.

Konundrum IV
Ketamine is infinite.

There are no boundaries to the effects of ketamine and there are no limits to what can be explored. You will always stumble across familiar places but the undiscovered country is vast beyond comprehension—larger than you could explore in a thousand lifetimes. The molecule is tiny but you can easily get lost in there. Many people do.

Konundrum V
Ketamine gives insights that sound like delusions.

Anyone who's taken ketamine knows what I'm talking about here. Ketamine has the power to make the impossible seem real and the intangible seem manifest. It imparts wisdom on cosmic, sub-conscious, genetic, and quantum levels. However, ketamine's particular gnosis simply transcends language and cannot be adequately translated without coming out sounding like gibberish. The knowledge gleaned is real enough, but it can never be verbalized or repeated. It is both a blessing and a curse.

Konundrum VI
Ketamine is warm and loving while being cold and heartless.

Ketamine will wrap you in a blanket of shimmering warmth while simultaneously sucking you dry. It will make your chi burn with the passion of a thousand suns while transforming your body into a shivering wreck. It will caress you softly with the care of a lover while extracting your soul with the cold efficiency of a machine. It is super-logical and sub-emotional, and attempting to pin it down as one or the other is futile. It can be all things to all people, and that's what's so powerfully attractive and dangerous about it. It can be both a doorway and a trap; it's up to you.

There is no doubt that ketamine is a teacher, but it is definitely not a plant teacher nor is it a particularly kind teacher. The lessons learned from ketamine are endless, but so is the toll it can take. Those who enter the world of ketamine without knowing what they want from it, or who fail to leave once they've found what they were looking for, will almost certainly be lost.

James Kent
—Publisher, *TRP*

INTRODUCTION

Ketamine has been around for over thirty years, but was relatively unknown to the general public until the 1990s when it was deemed one of the date-rape drugs. There is a lot of misunderstanding about what ketamine is and what it does. Those who are familiar with it and its effects are quick to point out that it is an extremely potent and fascinating drug. Ketamine's effects on the mind are so extraordinary that it may well replace LSD as one of the most controversial drugs of all time.

It is easy to imagine an entire subculture springing up around ketamine. The drug's potential influence on music, art, and social culture is incredibly powerful. Moreover, ketamine's impact on the brain's thinking processes can alter forever the way one views oneself, society and the universe. Efforts to pass and enforce laws to control ketamine have been more complicated than that of other drugs, such as LSD or ecstacy, because ketamine is recognized for its medical value and is used daily by plastic surgeons, among others, and veterinarians throughout the world. It is one of the few drugs on the "psychedelic" list—maybe the only one—manufactured legally by pharmaceutical companies.

The Little Book Of Ketamine demystifies ketamine for the non-scientific reader. There are many research papers that explain aspects of ketamine, but most are lengthy and difficult to comprehend without having a technical background in medicine. There are autobiographical works which share personal experiences with the drug. Although interesting, these books do not really get to the meat of the matter— the information most people are seeking about what ketamine is and what it can do.

The Little Book Of Ketamine is written in a clear, concise manner. It is candid and direct in describing all the fundamental facts of ketamine. The book discusses what ketamine is, how it works in the body and on the brain, how it affects the mind and what it feels like to go to K-Land. It describes how users prepare for a safe, conducive trip and how they handle ones that go astray. Readers will find information on how ketamine is packaged, sold and consumed. Finally, *The Little Book Of Ketamine* covers the history of ketamine, social concerns and the current laws, while being mindful of what is myth and what is reality.

Chapter 1

History Of Ketamine

Ketamine hydrochloride is known on the street as K, Ket, Kit-Kat, Special K, Super K, and Vitamin K. The FDA has approved ketamine as a general anesthetic for use on humans, especially with delicate patients such as children and the elderly. But it is most commonly used by veterinarians and plastic surgeons who conduct operations in their office. In recent years, it has become an increasingly popular recreational drug.

An american pharmacist named Calvin Stevens created CI581 in 1962, which was eventually renamed ketamine. Ketamine is an arylcyclohexylamine, and the most infamous member of that group of drugs is phencyclidine, known as PCP. While experimenting with arylcyclohexylamines in 1965, pharmacologists discovered that ketamine could be used as a safe general anesthetic because it is quick-acting and its psychoactive reactions are less pronounced than those produced by PCP. These attributes, plus its fast recovery period, made ketamine a perfect anesthetic to use in field hospitals during the Vietnam War.

Ketamine was patented in 1966 by Parke-Davis for use as an anesthetic in humans and animals. Early studies of ketamine's effects revealed dreams, trips, and a sense of well-being after using it. Hospital staff who participated in these early experimental trials carried word of "K's" recreational potential into the community.

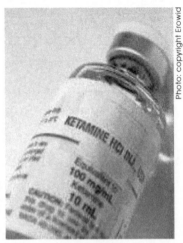

Photo: copyright Erowid

Ketamine HCL

Recreational Use

First documented accounts of recreational use of ketamine appeared in 1965 when it was described as a potent psychedelic drug by Professor Edward Domino, who coined the description "dissociative anesthesia" to describe ketamine's trance-like effects. Ketamine entered the pop drug culture by many routes. Dr. Karl Jansen, M.D., Ph.D., interviewed hundreds of ketamine users as part of his research. He tells a story about a heroin addict who found "this stuff called Ketalar" when he burgled a veterinarian clinic in the 1970s. Like many drug burglars, he routinely injected anything labeled "psychoactive." A few minutes later, he found himself "floating somewhere above the roof". After that, the addict said he was always looking for more.

Interest in ketamine spread quickly worldwide to London, Sweden, and Australia. Karl Jansen reports that in the mid-1970s, ketamine was already being used in Argentina to regress clients back to the womb so that they could be "born anew". Many veterans, having undergone surgery in battlefield hospitals, returned with stories about unusual psychedelic experiences while on the operating table. If you listen to one-liners delivered in the television comic series *M*A*S*H*, you can sometimes hear reference to ketamine.

Some recreational drug users were introduced to ketamine by the popular underground comic characters, *The Fabulous Furry Freak Brothers*. In one strip, the rock band "The Spoons" offers the fabulous threesome some lines of powder, which they snort, thinking it is cocaine. The Spoons then diabolically reveal that it is actually ketamine and tell the Freak Brothers that it causes a three-day nightmare. The final frame shows the trio pursued by various beasts and monsters as they make a hasty getaway in their hippie van. While this depiction was a misrepresentation of ketamine's effects, it spread myths about it. The ketamine experience can sometimes be like a nightmare, but its duration is brief, about an hour, not three days, for example.

Ketamine is widely used in Moscow, where the street scene is "hard-core," with a preference for intravenous injection over intramuscular injection or snorting crystals. Massive consumption of ketamine is common among Russian teenagers. Russian doctors sometimes prescribe ketamine as a pain-killer for the seriously ill. Karl Jansen reports a story about a little old lady selling K on the street for a few extra rubles.

Ketamine Goes Mainstream

The 1978 publication of autobiographical accounts in *Journeys Into The Bright World* by Marcia Moore and her husband Dr. Howard Alltounian, M.D., and *The Scientist* by Dr. John Lilly, M.D. titillated thousands of readers with

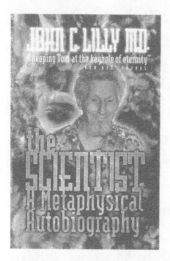

The Scientist is John Lilly's "metaphysical" autobiography.

personal stories of this new and fascinating drug experience.

Ketamine spread from the New York and California coasts inward. Ketamine was added to the DEA's "emerging drugs list" in 1995. They issued warnings in 1997 about the increase in ketamine abuse. In 1999, ketamine was scheduled by the federal government, thereby making nonprescription possession and use illegal. By the turn of the century, ketamine had moved into the mainstream with the growth of techno clubs and raves. Karl Jansen calls it a "global village event."

Not A Party Drug

Many ravers think that ketamine is similar to ecstasy. But ketamine is the wrong drug for the rave and techno club scene. The loud, crowded conditions that dance clubs present are in complete opposition to the sought after effects of ketamine, which requires quiet solitude. That has not stopped the dancing and dosing at Twilo in New York and other clubs throughout the world. It is rumored that some party-goers have dosed their dates in order to take advantage of them sexually. Although this kind of abuse of ketamine is rare, it has been lumped in with date-rape drugs like Rohypnol®, also known as "roofies," "rochies," or "rope." Unfortunately the media coverage of these crimes has done more to promote the taking of ketamine than practically every other source.

There have been articles about ketamine in mainstream magazines such as *Time* and *Cosmopolitan*. Even an Alfred Hitchcock film, *Family Plot*, included references to ketamine. An episode of the popular television series *The X-Files* told the story of a doctor giving Agent Mulder ketamine in order to help him recover his memory. K had a role in the mega-movie *Armageddon*, and it is said that the character portrayed by Jodie Foster in *Contact* experienced a ketamine-like episode in the film. The band Chemical Brothers recorded a song titled "Lost in the K-Hole." And, some claim, Madonna's "Ray of Light" was created with ketters in mind.

Ket Slang

Ketamine has many nicknames that vary from city to city and country to country. They include: K, Ket, Kit Kat, Keller, Kelly's Day, Vitamin K, Vit K, Special K, Special la Coke, Super Acid, Super K, Blind Squid, Cat Valium, New Ecstasy, Psychedelic Heroin, Green, and Purple. Street lingo for K effects and experiences include: K-Hole, K-Land, Baby Food, and God.

A person who uses ketamine is often referred to as a K-Head or Ketter. A snorted hit of K is called a "bump."

Chapter 2

What is Ketamine?

Ketamine hydrochloride ($C1_3H_{16}CINO$) is a fast-acting, hallucinogenic, "dissociative" general anesthetic used in the treatment of both animals and humans. The anesthetic effect results from the patient being so "dissociated" and "removed from the body" that it is possible to carry out surgical procedures. This is different from the unconscious effects produced by conventional anesthetics. Ketamine is an excellent painkiller used by doctors and veterinarians in the United States in surgical procedures under the brand names Ketalar® or Ketaset® manufactured by Parke-Davis for humans and Fort Dodge Animal Health for veterinary ketamine products.

Most of the ketamine available on the street in the United States has been stolen from veterinary clinics and pharmaceutical supply houses. It has been estimated that up to 90 percent of the ketamine bought on the street has been stolen from medical sources.

Ketamine is available on the Internet from various countries, including Mexico and Thailand. In Mexico, ketamine is an over-the-counter drug and available in various strengths from most pharmaceutical supply houses for veterinarians. It is easily purchased at border towns and smuggled into the U.S. since guards are looking for more traditional drugs, like pot.

Ketamine induces a dissociative state described as the separation of the mind or ego from the bodily existence and causes the mind to hallucinate other realities. Other dissociatives include DXM, which is used in cough medicines like Robitussin®, dizocilpine, which is a toxic research drug called MK801, and nitrous oxide, which is better known as laughing gas.

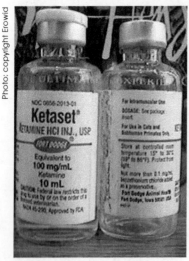

Ketaset® is manufactured by Fort Dodge and is used as an anesthetic by veterinarians.

The dissociative or out-of-body state is what many recreational users and spiritual adventurers are seeking when they use ketamine.

Medical Use Of Ketamine

Ketamine functions differently from most anesthetics. At higher doses it causes standard unconsciousness like any other anesthetic, but in lower doses the dissociative properties of ketamine cause out-of-body episodes, near-death experiences and alternate realities. Because many patients are frightened by such "head trips," doctors often combine a benzodiazapine, such as Valium® or other sedative, with ketamine to cause complete unconsciousness.

Ketamine is preferred by veterinarians and surgeons working out of private clinics because it is relatively safe compared to other anesthetics. It blocks the brain's nerve paths without limiting the patient's respiratory and circulatory functions, which means no support respiration is usually necessary. This allows physicians to perform surgical procedures as a "one-man operation" without assistance. Nonetheless, Parke-Davis cautions doctors in its fact sheet that Ketalar should be given to humans *only* by a specialist, in a hospital, with full resuscitation equipment available for those very rare cases when something does go wrong.

The breakthrough work of Dr. Karl Jansen, physician and psychiatrist, has demonstrated that ketamine can help prevent brain cell death in people in a severe life threatening crisis such as insufficient oxygen, extreme low blood sugar, and epileptic fits. An exciting developing use is with stroke victims. When ketamine is administered shortly after a stroke, there is mounting evidence that it can help reduce the severe brain damage associated with stroke.

Ketamine is used to treat trauma in young burn victims and, occasionally, in children's dentistry. The elderly, too, are sometimes administered ketamine for chronic pain.

Although users can build up a tolerance to K, studies show that it can suspend the development of tolerance and addiction to other drugs including heroin. Chronic pain clinics are known to use ketamine in combination with morphine to prevent tolerance to this pain-killer.

Psychotherapeutic Use

Since the mid 1980s, Dr. Evgeny Krupitsky, of the Leningrad Regional Dispensary of Narcology, has been researching the use of ketamine in the treatment of alcoholism. He has also announced his intentions to research ketamine's effects in post-traumatic stress disorder therapy.

It is doubtful, however, that ketamine can be very useful for psychotherapy, sometimes called the "talking therapy," because it interferes with cognitive functioning making meaningful communication practically impossible. Ketamine removes the person psychologically from the environment and the patient-client relationship. People on ketamine hardly relate! Karl Jansen says that other milder psychedelic drugs, like MDMA, ecstasy, and MBDB, Eden, might one day prove to be more suitable as aids to drug-assisted talking therapies.

Jansen points out that ketamine experiences, nevertheless, can have therapeutic—rather than psychotherapeutic—potential. The effects of the resultant altered state of consciousness itself can have a tremendous impact upon the person. It has been reported that near-death experiences associated with ketamine can have a favorable impact upon values, making people less concerned with material goals, for example. It also tends to reduce anxiety about death and has been linked to increased altruism. The experience can be a pivotal turning point, leading to positive life changes.

Psychotherapist Stan Grof, who researched psychedelics and their therapeutic effects for years, called ketamine "an absolutely incredible substance" and acknowledges that it offers remarkable philosophical and spiritual revelations.

Ketamine's impact upon the brain can promote mental health. Ketamine produces localized electrical abnormalities which may bear some resemblance to temporal lobe epileptic phenomena. Karl Jansen speculates that treatment with ketamine may have some effects resembling electro-shock treatment which is widely used in the United Kingdom to treat clinical depression. Researchers have reported that ketamine has some anti-depressant properties, as well.

There is indication that ketamine can help reduce fears and phobias. Two Iranian psychiatrists exposed patients to feared situations while under the influence of ketamine. They reported that many of the patients' fears were reduced sufficiently enough that they could be released from the mental hospital.

Another group of researchers gave ketamine to terminally ill patients to prepare them for death. The results were as predicted. The dying patients reported significant reduction in their fears of death.

A little known use of ketamine is as an anesthetic in state-mandated executions. In lethal injection execution, the prisoner is given three injections, the first is ketamine, the second two are lethal. Perhaps for these worst of criminals, dying is an estatic experience gratis the state.

Ketamine As A Psychedelic

Ketamine has hallucinogenic side-effects and there are numerous documented instances of abuse. Ketamine is a relative of phencyclidine or PCP, which are classified as arylcyclohexylamines. PCP is called "angel dust" on the street and has a reputation for "bad trips," psychotic episodes and even violence. Ketamine is far less toxic and its effects have a shorter duration than PCP. Violence in connection with ketamine use is exceedingly rare.

Ketamine is not a classic psychedelic drug like psilocybin, a chemical compound derived from

Ketamine's chemical name is Cyclohexanone, 2-(2-chlorophenyl)-2-(methylamino).

Source: Lyceaum

the mushroom *Psilocybe Mexicana,* or mescaline, which is obtained from the peyote cactus. Ketamine is not an amphetamine like DMT, MDA, and MDMA, nor is it a barbituate like Seconal® or Phenobarbital®. In fact, although Peter Stafford's *The Psychedelics Encyclopedia* has a good account of ketamine's basic effects, Stafford identifies as many as nine families of psychedelic drugs and ketamine is not among them.

The altered state of consciousness resulting from ketamine administration is very different from that produced by psychedelic drugs like LSD and DMT. On the other hand, the ketamine experience and acid trips do have similarities. Both produce vibrant hallucinations. A ketamine trip is usually a lot "heavier" than LSD, however, and more formidable. Even though the effects of ketamine are more potent and intense than LSD, the ketamine experience lasts only about an hour, whereas an acid trip is usually about eight hours. LSD has not demonstrated addictive qualities whereas ketamine can be highly psychologically addictive. When used frequently it can become life threatening because of the accidents which occur rather than any direct harmful effects of the drug. The dissociative effect of ketamine causes users to lose common sense thinking and ketamine users have drowned.

Timothy Leary characterized the ketamine experience as "experiments in voluntary death" and called it one of the most powerful psychedelics because it activated the highest circuit in his model of the nervous system—the neuroatomic circuit—that operates beyond space, time and the speed of light. Whereas LSD is a seventh circuit drug, Timothy Leary described ketamine as the "neurotransmitter" of the eighth neuroatomic circuit.

How K Works

Ketamine's dissociative effect causes users to experience a separation of the mind from the body. When this occurs, the senses become distorted and a new reality is created in the person's brain, rather than received from external stimuli and situations. Ketamine causes a wide range of effects beyond this distortion of the senses including hallucinations, out-of-body experiences and even near-death episodes.

Ketamine And The Brain

Ketamine blocks the action of the neurotransmitter called L-glutamate. When that happens, a particular brain receptor known as NMDA does not receive expected signals. NMDA receptors are involved in coordinating and integrating the conscious mind into all the bodily functions. They also interact with other parts of the brain.

It is hypothesized that before one can consciously experience a newly encountered experience, the receptors must have the "memory" of a similar, previous experience to relate to the new experience. When the signals are interrupted, the information bringing the new experience cannot be related to previous experiences, so the brain creates a new "reality."

Ketamine is thought to act on other receptors including the sigma receptor, where it combines with a nerve receptor causing it to potentially create a loss of contact with reality and normal social interaction. The PCP2 receptor, which influences serotonin levels, is also affected. This is where ketamine blocks a "reuptake channel" in much the same way as that the antidepressant drug Prozac® works.

Other reported brain reactions to ketamine include reduced brain wave activity and the production of brain wave patterns similar to those produced in a dream state. Rapid eye movement, which has also been associated with dreaming, often occurs. Ketamine increases excretion of the hormone epinephrine, known as adrenaline, into the bloodstream and releases beta-endorphins which are "feel good" hormones that bind to opiate receptors lessening pain and affect emotions. It is the combination of these processes that causes what Karl Jansen has labeled the "K-Trip."

K Stands For Knowledge

Awesome, mind-blowing, and overwhelming are just some of the ways users describe the extraordinary revelations ketamine generates. The thinking process under the influence of ketamine defies description. People report that the dissociative effect makes them embrace an unprejudiced or impartial viewpoint.

"I could see my thoughts," one K-Head explained. Another likened his experience to the early 1980s movie, *Tron*. "I felt as though I was stuck in this network or maze of electronic impulses. At first, I had no sense of being there, or rather, I was there and not there at the same time, a sort of annihilation of the ego." K-Trips have also been described as timeless, spaceless zones, where alternative universes "roll off the assembly line."

John Lilly believes he makes contact with extraterrestrials when high on ketamine. Perhaps the ability to view things objectively helps K-Users to see things from an alien's perspective! In his autobiography, Lilly described one of his experiences on ketamine:

> *I was a head on a flying carpet, flying through my mind, smiling. I was getting new Knowledge from K. K taught me so much in a very short period of time. It Knew everything. It said, "Everything ever Known is stored and can be visited." Also it said, "Knowledge starts with K for a reason." And many other tidbits of Knowledge. I asked it why I loved to trip so much, it said, "For the good of Man." Hmmm, I wasn't sure what that meant, but I Knew all along that it did have a purpose. K doesn't speak in audible words, it is like Knowledge implanted as you need to Know it. If you have a question that you've never been able to figure out, K will put the answer in your mind so you Know it. It is strange that way. Once you Know it, nothing can shake that out of you. You really Know it.*

Not all users feel as if they have entered different realities. Some connect to information networks, while others simply experience clear-sightedness and a greater understanding of life. Still others describe their experiences as contacting the higher self. Ketamine also produces "phase shifts" in which the person suddenly, without warning, goes from one "reality" to another.

DM Turner describes his experiences with ketamine in *The Essential Psychedelic Guide*:

> *Billions of images and perceptions are simultaneously flowing through my circuits. I am not bound into three dimensions. In the fourth dimension of time I am not locked into the current moment. I experience backwards and forwards in time as well, with the current moment being the center of intensity.*

Chapter 3

K-Trips

The peak of a K-Trip lasts from twenty minutes up to an hour. The "rush" can be pretty intense. So much so, that some people feel as if it literally takes their breath away. Intramuscular and intravenous users often hover at a semiconscious level for about an hour. Oral and nasal users experience this state for a somewhat longer period of time. The "coming down" period is rapid and, in a half-hour or so, the person regains control over the senses. The experience can proceed for another hour, perhaps as long as three hours, allowing the person an opportunity to refocus on our normal reality. This after-high is called the "soft trip."

Initially the person feels intoxicated and the room may spin. Confusion follows. It is common to have a sensation of labored breathing. Experienced users advise not to worry or overreact to it because the sensation will soon pass. If there is music playing, it will seem disjointed and louder than it actually is. Soon after, the person generally experiences a complete disassociation with the environment. If other people are present, the person high on ketamine will probably be unaware of them. It is during this period that people claim to experience different levels of being, visit alternate realities, observe unusual "patterns," and receive revelations of future events. These illuminating visions can become quite intense and, at times, frightening. Fright, however, is not an emotion people normally carry back with them to reality after a K-Trip.

DM Turner, who took ketamine more than 100 times and meticulously recorded his experience *The Essential Psychedelic Guide*, describes K-Tripping:

> *Some 30 minutes to an hour into the experience I come to an apex. At this point I have felt that my will determines whether or not I exist, and whether or not the universe exists. And I could toggle between existence and non-existence many times within a second. I've even had the impression that I could cause the universe, which is quite fluid in the moment, to crystallize in whatever format I desired, although I haven't had the impetus to actually try this.*

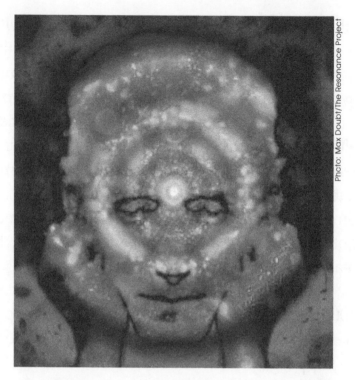

After this comes the return to regular consciousness, which begins with one perception out of each million seeming like it's within my familiar perceptual structure. These "personal perceptions" increase in frequency, one every 100,000, one every 10,000. Soon I remember my previous identity. I've never felt this moment as disappointing, as I frequently feel when coming down from ecstasy. When I realize I'm coming back it feels more novel like "Wow, I'm coming back, I wonder what life is going to be like after this

experience." Although there is a feeling that the ride's almost over, this part of the experience is quite interesting, with part of my mind still running circles around the cosmos, and another part reintegrating with my identity. Often I experience the return portion of the Ketamine journey as an alien rebirth experience.

Upon returning to the body, visuals will continue for a while with eyes closed. These can be quite spectacular and hallucinatory, and bear more resemblance to DMT visuals than other psychedelic visuals. 45 minutes to an hour after injecting the ketamine I'm back, though there remain some strange bodily sensations. I tend to feel light (anti-gravity), slightly dizzy, have poor motor coordination, and a bit nauseous if I move around. For a couple of hours after the experience I find it best to just relax, lay in bed, listen to music, etc. until the recovery period has passed.

The Mind And Body On Ketamine

Ketamine's effects differ from individual to individual. As with all drugs, people get out of it what they bring to it. Where one person may experience a kind of delirium, another may liken the effect to a revelation. Ketamine—as all drug experiences—is influenced by the four M's.

Makeup

What is the pharmacology of the drug? What is its purity level? Ketamine comes in two main forms: a white powder and a clear liquid. Sometimes it comes in capsule or pill form. Sometimes it comes wrapped in folded paper or aluminum foil. And sometimes it is packaged in small plastic bags or vials. Most commonly, ketamine comes in a sealed pharmaceutical vial which does not contain the impurities found in "street drugs."

Method

How is the drug taken? Is it smoked, swallowed, snorted, or injected? Ketamine can be taken by all of these methods in all kinds of doses, to achieve different levels of effects. Ketamine is normally take intramuscularly rather than intravenously. John Lilly injected himself 24 hours a day for several consecutive months without significant residual difficulties.

Mood

What is the person's psychological make-up and mental state when taking the drug? Other factors to consider are: intelligence, emotional stability, attitude, creativity, and the person's history of drug-taking.

One factor in the quality of the ketamine experience is personality. Dr. Igor Kungurtsev, a Russian psychiatrist, treated alcoholics with ketamine and confirmed a correlation between personality and nature of ketamine experiences. Negative experiences were associated with difficulty in relationships and having a controlling type of personality that fears letting go. Dissolution of self is a bummer for these folks. On the other hand, Kungurtsev found that people who are relaxed, able to surrender, and have a capacity to love find ketamine blissful, even ecstatic.

Motivation

Why is the person taking this drug? What are his or her expectations? Under what circumstances, conditions and setting is the drug being used—both physically and socially?

Raves are a bad place to take ketamine. In fact, taking it in any public place is generally discouraged. It is physically risky since the person usually becomes paralyzed and loses consciousness—except at low doses. Even so, coordination is diminished along with judgment and survival skills.

Taking the four M's into account, it becomes clear how reports of ketamine's effects stretch from strange, to wonderful, to unpleasant, to heavy, to hazardous.

When ketamine is administered at anesthetic levels, the person will enter what is known as a K-Hole or an unconscious state. In recreational use of ketamine, which is below anesthetic levels, the person is physically incapacitated, routine thinking is blocked, the senses are deadened and the memory dulled. Without external stimuli, the brain creates its own world in the form of hallucinations.

Ketamine's Effect

Ketamine has a powerful but short trip, lasting about an hour. It disconnects your mind and body from reality causing hallucinations, euphoria, a feeling of floating, and out-of-body experiences. As an anesthetic it eliminates all pain and sensory, and temporarily paralyzes the body. In high doses, it also causes unconsciousness.

Dissociation

Psychedelic journalist, Dan Joy says that the key to ketamine experience is dissociation. The tripper assumes a different point of view, one outside the body, outside the ordinary self and everyday concerns, even outside space and time.

Hallucinations

The medical establishment refers to hallucinations as "emergence reactions." Ketamine blocks or short-circuits the chemical messengers in the brain that transport sensory input, producing vivid hallucinations and other visual distortions, including tunnel vision. When the brain is blocked from sensory input it floods the "nothingness" with whatever is available. Visions come from within, sometimes taking the form of memories in dreamlike sequences. They are usually more observable in settings where the light source is very low. K-Heads have described contact with the dead, telepathy, ability to see the future, and magical events.

In addition to the dissociative phenomena, Dan Joy says that other common experiences include jacking into information networks in a ketamine cyberspace, interaction with alternative realities, and communication with extraterrestrials and disembodied entities.

Hearing

Ketamine narrows range of hearing so that frequencies are lost, while increasing volume. Because ketamine diminishes the bandwidth it is not a good drug for listening to music. Music can be intrusive and detract from ketamine's sought after effects. Many people report ringing, buzzing, humming, and whistling sounds in their ears.

Speech

People on ketamine do not generally feel like talking. When one does speak it is usually slurred. Repetition of a single word and nonsensical rhyming is also common. John Lilly made a famous tape, which can be heard on his web site, of the word "cogitate" repeated over and over. As you listen, it changes in strange and fascinating ways—and this is without being high on ketamine.

Smells And Tastes

Ketamine numbs taste and smell. Trippers are usually not interested in food, which is fortunate because experts caution that people should not eat or drink during a K-Trip for at least four hours beforehand.

Touch

Some people say they experience heightened sexual pleasure in the post-K state. Most people lose bodily sensations altogether. They feel numb and experience no pain. This is expected since ketamine was developed as an anesthetic.

Some people report enhanced sexual experiences. Dan Joy interviewed a ketamine user called Doctor Tantra who reported "the best place to take K is in bed with someone you love. It's a great way to play doctor. The mingling of energy fields is terrific. Just as LSD and nitrous oxide is a four-minute crash course in Bhakti Yoga, K is a lesson in Tantra." Once, under a combination of MDMA and K, he and his lover both hallucinated that they were making love passionately. When they came down from the trip, they discovered that they were fully clothed and had merely been touching fingertips! Other people report diminished interest in sex while under the influence of ketamine.

Emotions

Many people report mental confusion, euphoria, and "a warm feeling about the world." Having a sense of enlightenment is a common experience on ketamine.

Amazing Dope Tales by Stephen Gaskin

Electric Buddha

Sense of Time

Time slows down and eventually dissolves completely giving one the sense of eternity. It has been noted that the mind enters a "quantum" sea, beyond time and space.

Motor Skills

Like PCP, Quaaludes® and alcohol, ketamine makes the person feel lightheaded or drunk. As expected, the higher the dose, the more drunk one feels. Drowsiness, dizziness, nausea, and even vomiting have also been associated with the ketamine experience. Walking is practically impossible, and if one does manage to get upright, walking is robot-like. Even standing is difficult. Overall numbness and temporary paralysis is common. Many experience loss of memory spanning the period they were under the influence.

Mental Acuity

Memory of the experience is usually difficult. It is hard to bring back and integrate the ketamine experience with routine reality. The ketamine experience is bizarre and otherworldly. DM Turner theorized that a part of the mind protectively closes off access to the dimensions experience on ketamine. He found

a method that was effective in solving this problem, which was to take ketamine when already
high on 2-CB because it provides a "bridge"
between the ego or identity, and a state that is
ego-less and without limitations.

Other Effects

Other effects can include increased blood
pressure, decreased heart rate, vomiting, com-
bative or belligerent behavior, spasms, respiratory depression, convulsions, temporary paralysis, and unconsciousness. At higher doses, effects can include oxygen starvation of the brain
and muscles. An overdose can cause the heart
to stop completely.

Short Term After Effects

Other than feeling tired, probably over-
whelmed and maybe a little wobbly, most
people carry on normally day the following a
K-Trip. There have been reports that ketamine's
"come-down" can be "heavy." Again, it depends on how much and the manner in which
the it is taken.

Long Term Effects

There have been reports that ketamine im-
pacts vision and causes flashbacks. Inability
to concentrate and memory loss can occur. Psy-

chological dependence and the possibility of developing a psychosis are dangers in using ketamine.

Tolerance to ketamine develops quickly in repeated use. As tolerance builds, the duration of the trip is reduced, so more ketamine is required to reach the desired "high." Total resistance can develop so that the desired high is no longer accessible. As often happens with "tolerance," even when ketamine has not been used for long periods of time, the quality of the first-time high is never quite achieved again. When the person resumes ketamine intake, the same tolerance level is quickly reached.

With persistent long-term use, the effects of ketamine become less psychedelic and more like a mixture of opium, cocaine, marijuana and alcohol. Some heavy users report that ketamine mirrors the effects of amphetamines.

When using ketamine, much of the life energy know as chi or kundalini, departs from the body during the journey, normally returning along with one's awareness. With indiscriminate use, people return to find their body drained of this force. It is common to feel drained of energy or lackadaisical after a K-Trip.

Chapter 4

Shamanic Explorers

Ketamine has such a powerful impact that some people virtually devote their lives to its exploration, which is a seductive and dangerous pursuit. The allure is tremendous. A few have left behind maps of the allusive and fascinating K-Hole.

High Priestess Of Goddess Ketamine

Marcia Moore was a Harvard graduate, renown astrologer, therapist, and yoga instructor who, in 1976, began experimenting with ketamine. She affectionately called it the "aesthetic anesthetic" and claimed it was a key to the psycho-spiritual renaissance of the world. One of earliest discussions of the effects of ketamine is Moore's autobiography *Journeys Into the Bright World*, co-authored with her physician husband Dr. Howard Alltounian, in which she describes herself as the Priestess of the Goddess Ketamine.

Moore is credited with identifying the stages of the ketamine experiences. She called the highest state "cosmatrix," to describe the basic energy source from which all things are born. Moore documented the differences and similarities between ketamine and LSD, describing how some people experienced psychedelic effects while others did not, how continued use produced alternate personalities, and how tolerance built up.

Like many ketamine addicts, Moore used ketamine several times a week, each time with multiple injections. She documented her tolerance as it developed. After that, she established a routine of low-dose, pre-dinner sessions. Moore reported less need for sleep and more need for silence and solitude. Within a few months she was sleeping only about three hours a night.

While her husband begged her to stop using ketamine his pleas were futile. Moore continued obtaining ketamine from the supplier with his medical license number. She would sneak outside the house to secretly use it where her husband would not see her.

John Lilly, who was very aware of the dangerous side of ketamine after his own frightening experiences and the deaths of two people from his study group, warned Moore of ketamine's perils, but his advice went unheeded. At the age of 50, two years after she began her romance with ketamine, Moore vanished one night in 1979, never to be seen alive again.

For a year after her disappearance, her husband searched for her, including going to places she had traveled to like Hong Kong and Thailand. In the spring of 1981, Marcia Moore's bleached skeleton was discovered curled up in the crook of a tree where she had apparently frozen to death. It was her favorite place to sit while she injected herself with ketamine. Her husband, in a 1998 interview conducted by Karl Jansen, said that she became "addicted to ketamine and committed suicide." Jansen believes the evidence is more suggestive of an accidental death because she did not leave a note and there was no indication that she was depressed or wished to die.

DM Turner

Thought of as a shaman by many in the psychedelic community, DM Turner experimented regularly with various doses and combinations of psychedelic drugs. Being meticulous in everything he did, Turner kept detailed notes which he eventually self-published as *The*

Essential Psychedelic Guide—a basic how-to of psychedelic tripping with doses and cautions. Subsequently Turner published a second equally daring book, *Salvinorin — The Psychedelic Essence of Salvia Divinorum.*

Ketamine was Turner's fatal attraction—a love affair, gone wrong. He admitted that he was addicted to ketamine. You can feel the intensity of his romance with ketamine in the description of K-Tripping from his book.

> *As the high is coming on there is a break in the continuity of consciousness. Soon after this point I find myself in a swirling psychedelic universe. There is no concept that I am currently high on a drug that I'm going to come down from. Frequently there is no recollection of ever having been myself, been born, had a personality or body, or even know of planet earth. There experience is one of being in total orgasm with the universe. I feel like I'm in hyperspace, simultaneously connected to all things. . . .*
>
> *On my first Ketamine experience there was a non-verbal feeling that my entire life up to that point had been preparation, par-*

The Essential Psychedelic Guide
by DM Turner

ticularly my other psychedelic experiences, and taking Ketamine was like pressing the GO button. It felt as though there had been a major and permanent shift in the "fabric of reality" or the mode in which I perceived the universe. It felt as though the states of mind that I had broken through to in previous psychedelic peaks had become the base reality.

And this new reality felt better than I'd ever anticipated it could be. My past psyche-

delic experiences taught me how to release and flow within this type of world. On a Ketamine experience I do not need to "do" anything. Once administered, the experience simply happens. Sometimes I feel like a single atom or point of consciousness adrift in a swirling vortex of energies, like a single cell within a being of galactic proportions. This feeling may shift and I then become the center point through which all these energies pass. The experience is of titanic proportions in the merging of energy, intent, and awareness, yet lucidly articulated to the minutest spiraling details.

All the while I feel very relaxed and at home in this universe. Even though any supports of reality, identity, or stability are being dissolved at the speed of light, I do not experience any fear, as if the one who would experience fear at losing these things is not a part of me. As the waves of experience pass though me I feel a bit like a kid on a roller coaster. Although he's about to have an exhilarating experience while going over a hill, deeper in his mind he's confident that the roller coaster will stay on its tracks.

After struggling with his addiction for a few years, Turner believed he had it under control by allowing himself to K-Trip only as a reward for having accomplished something important. Over the course of his affair with ketamine, Turner's opinion of it changed. He came to think of it as a sort of "Frankenstein molecule" that did not obey the shamanic rules. Turner confided to friends that he had been given several warnings while tripping on mescaline and DMT to drop ketamine from his shamanic explorations.

The most intense message came when I tried combining ketamine with mescaline. When one takes a natural psychedelic like mescaline, they often come into contact with an age-old entities of that realm. With mescaline I find that I become a branch of a living entity, often called "Mescalito", who has existed at least since humans first ingested psychoactive cacti.

Mescalito can be viewed as being a conglomeration of the experiences of all mescaline users. It feels as though when taking mescaline I become an "eye" of Mescalito, and that he experiences through me. Mescalito has experienced much during his 3000+ year life time.

However, my introducing him to a powerful synthetic anesthetic/psychedelic left him shocked, stunned, and confused. It was a serious insult on my part to force this experience on Mescalito, especially since omens were telling me I should not do it.

He did not heed the warnings. Early in 1997, Turner was found dead in a bath tub in his home. Although no one really knows what happened, it is believed that Turner "rewarded" himself with a ketamine trip on New Year's Eve and that, at some point, while exploring hyperspace his earthly body slid under the water to quietly drown. The roller coaster jumped the tracks and Turner did not come back this time.

Turner left no will. He was only 34 years old and was not planning on dying so soon. With no designated heir to his literary properties, control of his life's work is in the hands of his family who, apparently, wish to suppress it along with his birth name.

Chapter 5

Scientific Explorers

Ketamine has opened new frontiers into the human brain, psyche, and spiritual awakening. Scientists are discovering how ketamine affects the brain, while discovering new things about the brain using ketamine.

John Lilly

Dr. John Lilly, M.D. is one of the Twentieth Century's most intriguing individuals. His life and work have been the inspiration for two popular movies *Day of the Dolphin* in 1973 and *Altered States* in 1980.

Lilly conducted pioneering research in biophysics, computer theory, electronics, neuroanatomy and neurophysiology. Timothy Leary called him "some sort of wizard, a science-fiction starman, a unique back-to-the-future alchemist." It is as a neuroscientist that Lilly is best known; mostly for his invention of the sensory deprivation—or isolation—tank, and for his communication experiments between human beings and dolphins.

During his early work studying the brains of monkeys and other animals, Lilly mapped the pain and pleasure centers of the brain. This work was subsequently used by the military to create live animal bombs,

John Lilly did in-depth studies on the psychedelic effects of ketamine using first-hand experimentation.

delivered by zapping their pleasure and pain centers. When donkeys, equipped with bombs strapped to their bodies, got off course while walking a narrow trail over the mountains to the enemy, they were zapped in the pain center putting them back on course. This twisted use of his discoveries effected Lilly traumatically, propelling him to drop out of establishment research to launch into self-experimentation with LSD and ketamine.

In the course of this work mapping brains, Lilly inserted 610 electrodes into the cerebral cortex of a macaque monkey's brain. Years later as he became deeply involved with ketamine, he became obsessed with the image of hundreds of electrodes in the monkey's brain. In his autobiography, he describes his desire to put electrodes into his own brain because he felt ethics required that he do to himself what he did to his patients—the monkeys.

> *Then eventually I will use myself as the subject of the experiment . . . . Until one is willing to undergo the experiments oneself, one must not perform them on other humans. I will oppose those who use patents as experimental subjects before they use it themselves. A doctor should never give a drug to a patient until he has tried it himself. A doctor should not insert brain electrodes in patients until he is willing to insert them in his own brain. I visualize ten thousand, a hundred thousand, a million electrodes inserted through my skull into my own brain, hooked up to an adequate recording system.*

Lilly did not put real electrodes into his brain, of course. Instead, he explored his brain with a sort of ketamine electrode. His autobiography, *The Scientist,* first published in 1978, spread the word about ketamine and its effects probably more than any other source. In it, he explains how he was given ketamine by a physican named Craig Enright in the 1970s to treat chronic migraine headaches. Lilly reports that his headaches stopped. Being a physician himself, he had unlimited access to ketamine and it was not long before he was taking it on a daily basis, often for long periods of time. He said it enabled him to "look across the border into other realities," and to venture beyond "the social consensus reality" to more profound "meta-realities."

Floating in the "Lilly Tank," which is an enclosed bath-sized tank filled with heavily salted warm water, enabled him to achieve dissociative states and out-of-body experiences without ketamine. For a time in the 1970s and early 1980s, the sensory deprivation tank—or floatation tank, as it was alternatively called—was manufactured and sold to enthusiasts who reported being profoundly relaxed after the experience. Always an extremist, however, Lilly pushed the envelope by taking large doses of ketamine and spending hours in the tank. His harrowing experiences are chronicled in *The Scientist* and *The Center of the Cyclone.*

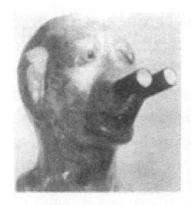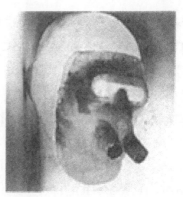

John Lilly had breathing masks made to allow him to spend hours submerged in the deprivation tank.

Some call Lilly a visionary; others say he went too far. On one occasion, after injecting ketamine, he was found face down, unconscious in his swimming pool. Lilly's use of ketamine was often excessive. He describes how over a three week period, he injected 50 milligrams of ketamine every hour, nearly 24 hours a day. While doing so, he became convinced that he was a visitor from the year 3001 or alternatively, that a being from the year 3001 had taken over his body.

Lilly's self-experimentation demonstrated that chronic ketamine use leads to hazardous levels of "automatism," in which the person experiences the body like a machine separate from consciousness and eventually goes into a coma. On three separate occasions, he was diagnosed with a paranoid psychosis and hospi-talized. Lilly describes one incident in *The Center of the Cyclone* where he tried to call Gerald Ford, then-President of the United States, to caution him about what he perceived as "the intervention in human affairs of the solid-state life forms elsewhere in the galaxy." Lilly believed he could speak with extraterrestrials who traveled to earth to choreograph coincidences to gently push mankind down the evolutionary path.

When asked in a 1998 interview with *USA Today* about the possibility of legal controls on ketamine, the then 82-year-old Lilly argued that it was an overreaction because ketamine "allows you to explore the depths of the mind." On other occasions, however, he agreed that ketamine is "dangerous if you don't know what you're doing" and should be restricted.

Karl Jansen

Karl Jansen, M.D., Ph.D., London psychiatrist and researcher, is the world's leading scientific expert on the non-medical use of ketamine. He was born in New Zealand, where he attended the University of Auckland to became a medical doctor, graduating with high honors. While at the university, he began his studies into the mind/brain interface for which he was awarded the prestigious Fowlds Memorial Prize in Medicine and Human Biology.

Subsequently, Karl Jansen went to the United Kingdom where he completed advanced training in clinical pharmacology and psychiatry. He is a member of the Royal College of Psychiatrists. It was while he was conducting this early brain research that Jansen became interested in ketamine. Since then, he has been fascinated how ketamine reproduces near-death-like experiences, such as lights, tunnels, and visions of God, and he is also studying ecstacy (MDMA) and other dance drugs.

Karl Jenson's inquiries into the effects of ketamine span every level, from photo-imaging receptors in the brain to which ketamine binds, to investigating how K-Trips (a term he coined) resemble near-death experiences and open doors to other realities, to uncovering ketamine's potent healing powers when employed in a theraputic setting, to developing methods to treat ketamine addiction. He is extending these methods into other areas of mental health to develope a revolutionary approach to mental health care he calls "quantum psychiatry."

Included in Jansen's research are interviews with hundreds of ketamine users about their experiences. For example, he interviewed Lilly, who was 83 years old at the time, and found his mental state to be "in pretty fine shape, all things considered."

Jansen's Glutamate Theory

Karl Jansen is a pioneer in pointing to the importance of the glutamate system in the brain. As he explains it, the brain contains natural drugs to protect it from cell death. Under special circumstances, these natural brain chemicals have ketamine-like effects. They seem to be responsible for dreaming, and may play a key role in brain disfunctions such as schizophrenia.

Glutamate, an excitatory amino acid, is a neurotransmitter used by most neurons in the higher brain. Its action is of central importance in the brain. Jansen says that it is glutamate that makes us "human and unique." When present in excess, however, neurons become over-excited and die in a process called "excitotoxicity." Blockage of the PCP receptor, which is also the receptor for ketamine, prevents cell death from excitotoxicity. Life threat-

Dr. Karl Jansen is the leading researcher of ketamine, its effects and potential benefits.

ening situations, like insufficient oxygen and low blood sugar, trigger a glutamate flood which damages or kills brain cells. Jansen's "glutamate theory" postulates that ketamine-like substances naturally present in the brain work to prevent this damage, thereby preserving the brain. His research points to near-death experiences as being a "side effect" of these chemical actions—albeit with enormous spiritual and psychological potential.

Jansen says ketamine administered by intravenous injection is capable of reproducing all of the features of the NDE and that this is not simply an interesting coincidence. "This discovery led me to the prediction that the brain would have a natural protective mechanism against the glutamate flood, probably a counter-flood of natural tunnel blockers producing K-Like psychedelic effects. While a person is having a near-death experience (NDE), the brain is preserving itself from damage. And this kind of cell death can be prevented by administering ketamine. The degree of damage and the mental state which result depend on the balance between toxic (glutamate) and protective (K-Like substance) forces, a kind of battle between good and evil played out at the chemical level. It must be emphasized again," Jansen continues, "that K itself is not found in the brain naturally, and it is not glutamate which has the NDE-like effects."

Jansen explains that ketamine binds to the receptors that play important roles in thinking, memory, emotion, language, sensation and perception, causing a blockage in the flow of current. "K changes the way in which incoming data is integrated or blocks it out altogether, isolating parts of the brain from the setting. The usual players are cleared from the stage, which is then filled with new realities originating in the depths of the mind." There are chemicals which occur natually in the brain which can also do this, like when you are dreaming. He concludes that near-death experiences are "the final common result of several causes, not a single cause which always operates."

In general, Karl Jansen feels that some near-death experiences are the same as ketamine-induced visions, and insists that his ideas do not diminish spiritual and psychological meaning of near-death experiences. Quite the opposite. Jansen says he has become more interested in spiritual ideas as a result of his ketamine research and is expanding his empirical inquiries into the rebirthing aspects of K-Trips. Jansen's research is ongoing and he is constantly looking for ketamine users to add to his studies.

Jansen warns that ketamine is very addictive. He says ketamine is "a most potent, mind-shaking psychedelic drug, which has killed some people, driven others mad, caused addiction, causes hallucinations, and has qualities which are like a powerful combination of heroin, cannabis and cocaine all rolled into one." In spite of its high potential for abuse, he wonders that ketamine is regulated as only a Schedule III drug, whereas marijuana is tightly regulated as a Schedule I substance. Jansen questions the apparent absurdity and points out that "ketamine is pumped into children as an intravenous infusion in huge doses, sometimes for days. It can even be ordered in the mail," and he wonders "why." Considering the possible answers led him to become interested in what Timothy Leary calls "the politics of ecstasy." "Having spent too many years under the low grey skies of England," watching "the puppet strings being firmly pulled by the large drug companies for whom the police, media and politicians are simply hired hands," is disturbing. So much so that he gloomily relabeled it "the economics of hypocrisy."

Like Lilly, Karl Jansen also became disillusioned. Eventually he left Oxford and went to the world's leading institution for psychiatric research, the Maudsley and Bethlem Royal Hospitals and London Institute of Psychiatry, where he continues his research.

Chapter 6

Spiritual Explorers

Ketamine is a powerful entheogen, which is a term coined by Jonathan Ott, an ethnobotanical researcher, to describe substances with the capacity to generate inner experiences of Gods, gods, or divinity.

For many people, spirituality is the key component of the ketamine experience. They consider it a shamanic experience that gives deeper understanding of their role in the universe. They usually have out-of-body episodes and may even undergo near-death and rebirth-type experiences. Astral projection is common.

Some researchers believe the spiritual experiences occurring during acid trips result from acid's interaction with the neurotransmitter serotonin, which is a major factor in regulating mood. Serotonin derives from tryptophan, which is found naturally in cocoa, bananas, and turkey. Ketamine, on the other hand, produces its effects by blocking L-glutamate. Other psychedelics like LSD cause sensory overload and, therefore, a great awakening is often achieved. People become more aware of the expanding universe and gain the ability to focus on minute details. The ketamine experience, by contrast, is often death-like, with an external sensory shutdown and move toward an inner universe.

Yet, both LSD and K can result in transcendental experiences of "oneness." With both, the person experiences a loss of ego. On LSD, you may see God—or even become God. On ketamine you will probably have "telepathic synergistic" communications with God. For ketamine users, the experience feels so authentic that they may believe that they actually left their bodies.

Igor Kungurtsev, the Russian psychiatrist who treated alcoholics with ketamine, found that it produced spiritual experiences and changed the spiritual outlook of most people he studied. Many of his patients

Photo: Osyrus, copyright Erowid

Ketamine users have reported feelings of spiritual awakening as a result of out-of-body experiences.

never thought about spirituality or the meaning of life. He said, "For many patients it is a profound insight that they can exist without their bodies as pure consciousness or pure spirit." Many of them said that as a result of their experience, they understood the Christian notion of the separation of the soul and the body, and that they now believe some part of them will continue to exist after death. There were several cases where people reported contact with God, but this is usually not an anthropomorphic figure. They describe an ocean of brilliant white light, which is filled with love, bliss, and energy.

Near-Death Experiences

One of the effects ketamine users often encounter is called a "near-death experience" (NDE). The most notable feature of near-death experiences is the feeling of leaving the body. The experience is beyond words and cannot be described using language. There is a sense of timelessness, analgesia, apparent clarity of thought and feelings of calm and peace. NDE's can be disturbing and frightening, however. People commonly hallucinate landscapes, partners, parents, teachers, friends, and especially

religious and mythical figures, including angels, and an awe inspiring light that is believed
to be God. The famed "life review" is rare,
however transcendental states are common.

Karl Jansen and other scientists have shown
that the intravenous administration of 50 to
100 mg. of ketamine can reproduce all of the
features that are commonly associated with
spontaneous NDE's, but events evolve at a
slower pace and last longer.

Many people have had experiences of leaving their body during lucid sleep—which is
remarkably similar to the ketamine experience
in some ways. In both, the person is mentally
lucid and aware, but un-
able to move. Robert Mon-
roe describes his early out-
of-body experiences in
Journeys Out Of The Body.
The Monroe Institute is
devoted to helping people
have out-of-body experi-
ences through use of psy-
chological techniques.

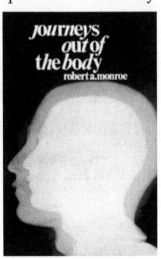

Raymond Moody, a
psychiatrist, coined the
term, "near-death experi-

Robert Monroe's book
about out-of-body
experiences.

ence," which he described in his book, *Life After Life*. The classic NDE occurs when one has a close brush with death, such as during surgery or when seriously injured. People report floating out of their body, seeing their lifeless form below and hearing what others are saying. They also report seeing an incredibly intense, but not blinding, white light that makes them feel safe and loved.

Other characteristics of the near-death experience include a feeling of calmness, lack of physical pain, crystal-clear thoughts, a perception that time is endless, and a sense of serenity or peace. Some people hear noises at the beginning, others are visited by dead loved ones. Still others have encounters with angels. The compelling feeling is of being connected to a powerful, beneficent power.

Ketamine And NDEs

Karl Jansen's research led him to theorize that the similarity between spontaneous near-death experiences and ketamine trips is due to the blockade of receptors in the brain. "A sudden fall in oxygen or blood sugar, which may result from interruption of the blood supply during a heart attack, has been shown to cause a flood release of glutamate," explains Jansen. "This over-excites brain cells which die, like bursting a balloon by over-filling it. K can prevent this brain damage via the same mechanism which produces K-Trips: blockade of tunnels so that the sea cannot rush in."

Jansen also emphasizes that having a near-death experience produced by ketamine does not mean that the person was physically near death. In fact, with ketamine, the heart rate actually rises instead of dropping. Jansen explains that a near-death experience can be divided into two normally contradictory parts. Jansen said:

> K is one of the most split drugs ever discovered. It takes some people much further in than they have ever been, and yet they may find themselves much further out. K is a source of both healing and harm, integration and disintegration—a set of balanced contradictions. Perhaps the brain can act as a transceiver, converting energy fields beyond the brain into features of the mind, like a TV converting waves in the air into programs. Quantum physics suggests that both K and the conditions which produce near-death ex-

periences may retune the brain to provide access to certain fields and broadcasts which are always there. The fact that near-death experiences can be induced does not imply that near-death experiences are unreal.

Chapter 7

Dosage And Use

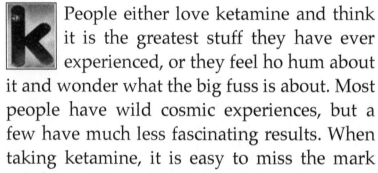People either love ketamine and think it is the greatest stuff they have ever experienced, or they feel ho hum about it and wonder what the big fuss is about. Most people have wild cosmic experiences, but a few have much less fascinating results. When taking ketamine, it is easy to miss the mark and have a disappointing experience.

The main consideration in maximizing the potential for a quality trip, according to DM Turner, is taking the correct dose. Too small an amount will not obliterate self-awareness, and will fail to take one to pure awareness. Too much ketamine brings on unconsciousness and throws the person into a K-Hole, leaving one with a vague impression of having traveled somewhere. Turner suggested starting with 75 mg. as an intramuscular injection and increase the doses by 15 mg. on each separate occasion until the desired result is reached.

Preparation

To snort or ingest a drug it must be in a powder form. With ketamine, this is accomplished by placing liquid ketamine in a spoon and holding it over the low heat of a stove in much the same way that heroin is "cooked." In an instant, the ketamine turns into tiny crystal granules. Larger batches are poured on a glass tray and set in an oven at 200 °F until the liquid evaporates. The powder that remains is scraped off. After it is chopped finely with a razor blade or through a grinder, the resulting powder is ready for use.

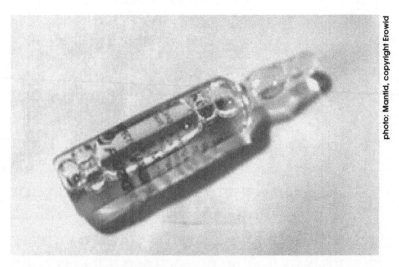

photo: Mantid, copyright Erowid

Ketamine is packaged in vials, such as this one, by pharmaceutical companies.

Some people make the powder into a drink by using a half-glass of warm water and, after stirring in the powder thoroughly, filling the rest of the glass with orange or another fruit juice to counteract ketamine's unpleasant taste.

Dosage Levels

Ketamine can be taken in various doses. A smaller dose allows one to maintain some sense of identity, memory, and ability to perceive and interact with the physical surroundings. Turner says that a 10 to 20 mg. dose put him into a non-psychedelic, dissociative altered semi-conscious halfway zone and 75 to 125 mg. usually produces the sought after K-Trip.

When dosing with ketamine, there is a point where people lose the ability to control their primary senses. This is referred to as a "line dose." There is another line that exists beyond this one called "anesthetic" where the person loses total consciousness.

Caution is needed when comparing doses of ketamine with ecstasy, cocaine, and speed. K is much more potent than any of these other drugs and taking too much of it causes unconsciousness. One veterinarian warns that less than one-half ounce of ketamine can tranquilize a horse!

Intramuscular and Intravenous Dosages

Turner says that a 100 mg. dose of ketamine taken intramuscularly produces an intense psychedelic experience. The Vaults of Erowid, an on-line library of information about psychoactives, spirituality, culture and law, has compiled detailed dosage information. Like most other drugs, different dosages of ketamine, relative to other factors, produce diverse effects.

Erowid Ketamine Dosages

Intra-muscular Doses

Threshold	.1 mg./lb.	10-15 mg.
Light	.15 mg./lb.	15-30 mg.
Common	.2 mg./lb.	25-50 mg.
Strong	.5 mg./lb.	40-100 mg.
K-Hole	75 mg./lb.	60-125 mg.
Anesthetic	1 mg./lb.	100-200 mg.
LD50 (IVN-MUS)	77 mg./lb.	~4,500 mg.
LD50 (IPR-MUS)	400 mg./lb.	~24,000 mg.

Intramuscular Administration

It is common to have muscle pain when injecting larger doses of liquid ketamine into muscle tissue. The pain can continue for several days if ketamine has not been administered properly. The muscle soreness is somewhat controlled by using a very fine, small gauge needle and by injecting very slowly. Properly injecting a ketamine dose into a muscle takes 15-30 seconds or more. Slowing down the injection rate reduces sting. Intramuscular and intravenous administration generally produce a higher peak, and a shorter overall duration than other methods.

Intramuscular Timing

Onset:	1-5 minutes
Duration:	45 minutes-1.5 hours
Back to Baseline:	T+4-6 hours
*LD50:	dose that kills an animal

Oral and Rectal Doses

Threshold	.3 mg./lb.	40-50 mg.
Light	.6 mg./lb.	50-100 mg.
Common	.75-2 mg./lb.	75-300 mg.
Strong	1.5-2.5 mg./lb.	200-450 mg.
Anesthetic	3-4 mg./lb.	500+ mg.
LD50 (IVN-MUS)	77 mg./lb.	~4,500 mg.
LD50 (IPR-MUS)	400 mg./lb.	~24,000 mg.

Oral Administration

An oral dose is prepared from a powder by placing the powder in a cup. About 1 cm. of hot water is poured into it and stirred to solution. The remainder of the cup is filled with an acid such as orange juice because ketamine tastes quite bad.

Oral Administration Timing

Onset:	5-20 minutes
Duration:	1.5 hours.
Back to Baseline:	4-8 hours.

Rectal Administration

A syringe with the needle removed is filled with the desired dose. A lubricant is used to help insert the syringe into the rectum, where it is injected. Rectal use is similar to oral in that it has a lower peak, but longer duration.

Rectal Administration Timing

Onset:	5-10 minutes.
Peak:	20-30 minutes
Duration:	2-3 hours.
Back to Baseline:	4-8 hours.

Nasal Doses

Threshold	.1 mg./lb.	10-15 mg.
Light	.15 mg./lb.	15-30 mg.
Common	.3 mg./lb.	30-75 mg.
Strong	.5 mg./lb.	60-125 mg.
The K-Hole	~1 mg./lb.	100-250 mg.
LD50 (IVN-MUS)	77 mg./lb.	~4,500 mg.
LD50 (IPR-MUS)	400 mg./lb.	~24,000 mg.

Nasal Administration

Nasal doses are highly unlinear next to oral and intramuscular doses. The effects are quite different at low doses. A low dose nasally will be short and much different from a comparable oral dose. The user snorts or "insufflates" 25 mg. in each nostril, waits 5 minutes, and snorts another 25 mg. in each nostril. This is repeated until the user reaches the desired dosage.

Nasal Administration Timing

Onset:	5-15 minutes.
Duration:	10-30 minutes.
Back to Baseline:	45-90 minutes, increasing with dose.

Reprinted by permission of The Vaults of Erowid, www.erowid.org

Variables like the size of the person's body and where and how it is taken influence the quality of the trip. The person's tolerance level and whether or not other drugs are taken in conjunction with ketamine are also important considerations. Keeping in mind that these are generalized parameters, Erowid's dosage charts describe measurements in mg. by the type of administration.

Combination Doses

DM Turner used himself as a subject in his extensive experiments combining ketamine with other psychedelics. He found that when he took ketamine while already high on a psychedelic, like 2-CB or LSD, the "dosage window" for achieving a desirable K-Trip is significantly wider. He found that ketamine combined best with 2-CB, producing an enhanced K-Journey while reducing the negative effects during the recovery period. He reported good experiences with some rare synthetic phenethylamines, including 2CT7, 2CT2, and DOB combined with ketamine. Turner found that combining ketamine with LSD produces an enhanced K-Journey, but the recovery period is "a serious drag."

Turner found that 2-CB and ketamine produces highs which are quite different. About taking this combination, Turner said, "it feels like two streams crossing at right angles" which produces a uniquely new universe of experience. He said that this combination works well with doses as small as 25 mg. or as large as 100 mg. of ketamine. With a small dose of ketamine, Turner reported no actual K-Trip, but felt "the relaxed immersion in flowing psychedelic mental fireworks" as very enjoyable.

When used with 2 CB, the ketamine recovery period is also diminished, with greater ease of movement, little feeling of nausea, and often a feeling of exceptional physical energy. "I have frequently emerged from the ketamine journey and immediately begun dancing about like a whirling dervish, or assuming yogic asanaas where intense subtle energies were transversing and harmonizing within my body," is how Turner described it.

Turner said 2-CB enabled him to build a bridge between normal reality and the bizarre and amazing world of ketamine. When he took ketamine with 2-CB he had increased recollection of the ketamine domain.

Chapter 8

Ketting Safety

K Ketamine is different from other psychedelics when it comes to safety because it has significantly greater hazards and pitfalls. Injection is usually involved, whereas other psychedelics are rarely injected. Physical activity can be precarious with any psychedelic but with ketamine it is extremely dangerous due to the tendency towards unconsciousness.

Physical Safety

The environment in which one experiences a ketamine trip is of vital importance. However, the choice of setting varies from person to person. There are a number of cautions that ketamine experts say are important to ensuring a fruitful experience.

Getting into a bath or hot tub should always be avoided to prevent drowning. Being where one could fall, such as sitting on a ledge, should be avoided. Of course, driving is extremely dangerous and should never be attempted during a K-Trip and for several hours afterward. Knowledgeable users are careful to extinguish all candles to avoid fire.

Turner advised that the K-Tripper have someone be in attendance who is not "Ketting" to act as a monitor, watching for potential problems. Lying down in bed or on a mat with a blanket for warmth is the safest and most comfortable position. Many people have a lot of soft pillows for added comfort. Interruptions are annoying and are limited by disconnecting the phone and not answering the door. Most people visit the bathroom beforehand. Food should never be eaten for at least 90 minutes prior to tripping, although not eating for four hours allows the stomach to completely empty. A container is usually nearby in case of vomiting.

Experienced K-Trippers emphasize the importance of programming oneself to not move for the duration of the trip. If moving is essential, the person must exercise extreme caution because coordination and vision are both severely impaired. Moving about during the first hour after shooting up, can cause nausea and vomiting. Because of the impaired coordination, experienced users caution that smoking cigarettes and joints should be avoided. It is easy to start a fire and in the ketamine impaired state, the person may not be able to get away.

Hearing is more sensitive under the influence of ketamine, so most people prefer no music or music that is slower, calming, background-type, new-age-style compositions. Music with a heavy beat intrudes on the K-Journey. Some people use tapes and CD recordings that last an hour so that they do not have to attend to it after they begin tripping. Additionally, people generally prefer low light or darkness which enhances the visual dimension of ketamine.

Addiction Potential

When a person feels unable to cope without ketamine, a state of psychological dependence has developed. Rick Doblin of the Multidisciplinary Association for Psychedelic Studies (MAPS) says, "Psychologically, it (ketamine) has an addictive potential that is greater than any of the other psychedelics." After DM Turner struggled with his own dependency, he came to think of ketamine as a kind of "psychedelic heroin." Unlike heroin and alcohol addiction, there is no physical discomfort when withdrawing from the drug.

Lilly and other ketamine users abhor the term "addiction." Lilly preferred his own terms, "the repeated use trap," and "seduction by K." Many K-Trippers find the experience so enjoyable that they use the drug constantly until their supply is used up. People who have had no problems controlling their use of pot, cocaine, or opium often go off the deep end with ketamine.

The danger of too much frequency or too big a dose is always present. Ketamine users do not know how much their brain can handle until they have gone too far. Experts warn that use should be done sensibly. People who do not plan their experiences in advance or who fail to stick to predetermined dosage levels can go beyond safe limits. Death is always a possibility when using ketamine.

Overdosing

The K-Hole where one becomes unconscious or comatose is life threatening. But death resulting from ketamine itself is rare. Lilly used ketamine numerous times a day for months without apparent physiological damage, although he nearly drowned while on ketamine. A person is more apt to die in an accident than from using ketamine—or so ketamine enthusiasts claim!

Madness

The possibility that a person might attempt "crazy" stunts, like trying to fly or exiting a moving automobile, increases the more often ketamine is taken. Ketamine is a powerful painkiller. A person high on ketamine theoretically can walk through a plate glass window, not feel it, and bleed to death. If they become nauseated, people can choke on their vomit due to being unable cough up because of temporary paralysis.

Ketamine can push people "over the edge" to trigger a drug-induced psychosis. Flashbacks might be a problem, but it has not been established how real these are or how common. Fatigue might trigger a K flashback, for example. Ketamine can cause other neurological and psychological disorders including depression and possibly seizures. Some people panic because they are afraid they will never come back to reality.

Feeling as if one has stopped breathing and panicking is common. Experienced ketamine users say that the odds of stopping breathing are low and advise that the best thing to do is to "go with the flow," because fighting the ketamine effects can actually trigger a bad experience.

Physical Distress

The dizzying effects of ketamine can cause vomiting and subsequent choking. Fortunately, the gagging and coughing reflexes remain in tact so that this is usually not a worry, since the person is unlikely to choke.

As with cocaine and crack, chronic users can create a hole inside the nose from snorting too much. Snorting can also impair the sense of smell. Some people experience stomach pain. A small percentage of people get a ringing sound in their ears called "tinnitus." There have been some reports of impotence.

Needle Safety

Another risk factor is that injecting anything, whether it is an illegal drug or diabetes medicine prescribed by a physician, it can have serious repercussions. The purity of the material and safe use of needles is paramount. Many people are understandably afraid of needles, but ketamine is actually much safer than "street drugs." Ketamine usually comes in a sealed pharmaceutical vial and does not contain the impurities often found in drugs made in a clandestine underground lab.

Health officials caution to use only new, sealed hypodermic syringes. Some large cities have needle exchange programs to facilitate this important issue. Syringes and needles are available over the internet, often without a doctor. For example medical supplies, from a thermometer to a box of gauge 26 needles or a box of 1,000 one ml syringes can be delivered to your door by courier within a few days from companies such as "Medistore." There are many other sites around the world which will deliver medical supplies to people's homes on re-

Photo: Max Doubt/ The Resonance Project

Medical supplies such as syringes and needles can be bought online without a doctor's prescription.

ceipt of a credit card number and address—no further questions asked. However, that does not mean that possession or use is unlawful. Readers are advised to update themselves on local laws and regulations and abide by them. Needles should never be shared, not even with a lover or close friend, because HIV, hepatitis, other infections and deadly diseases are spread by blood serum.

Dan Joy suggests that ketamine users inject themselves in the rump to avoid hitting a nerve. Many people inject into the thigh and upper arm. Karl Jansen says the upper arm is best for a clean injection and full absorption of one dose.

Contamination

Liquid ketamine usually comes in a sealed pharmaceutical vial which allows confidence in its purity. Knowing what one is getting and where it came from is always important. Anything procured at a club or rave should be viewed with suspicion. Sometimes drugs sold at these venues as K turn out to be cut with unknown substances, or not even K at all! Drugs frequently mixed with K include cocaine, ecstasy, and heroin. Injecting this kind of "underground" K is very risky. Drinking alcohol while on ketamine is always a bad idea.

Ketamine taken in smaller doses may allow the K-Tripper to maintain balance, possibly even to dance. However, heatstroke is a concern. People who use ketamine at raves at dance clubs should always drink a lot of water, take frequent breaks and keep cool. Any one of the following symptoms could be a sign of heatstroke: Headache or fatigue, lightheadedness, fainting, vomiting, cramps, and inability to sweat or urinate.

Bad Trips

A number of effects can manifest in people high on ketamine, including fear, panic attacks, anxiety, depression, thoughts of suicide, flashbacks, paranoia, delusions of grandeur, automatic behavior, multiple personalities, aggression and others. If a person is having a "bad" trip, there are several things that can minimize distress.

First, if the setting is noisy, such as a rave or frenzied night club, the distressed person should be encouraged to leave and to go to a more tranquil environment. A sober person should assist and watch over them. The attendant should not whisper, make exaggerated gestures, or act "suspicious," as K-Users can exhibit paranoid tendencies. "Head games" should be avoided with a person on a bad K-Trip. Speaking in a reassuring and direct manner is best. A distraught K-User should never be left alone. The ketamine impaired person could fall down stairs, for example, step in front of oncoming traffic, or could become the victim of rape. Ketamine represses the ego and if the person does not maintain a measure of identity, lapsing into unconsciousness is likely.

Brain Damage

There is no evidence that ketamine causes brain damage in humans or monkeys. Ketamine has been linked to brain damage in rats, the brain cells of which differ from humans. Although the rat research may not have any meaning for humans, some K-Heads endorse the use of sedatives along with ketamine in order to prevent brain damage. It apparently works on lab rats, so enthusiasts reason that it should work on humans, too.

A low dose of tranquilizers known as the benzodiazepines, which includes Valium® and Librium®, is considered much safer than barbiturates, such as Seconal®, which can be deadly. They do protect some brain cells and, in turn, also heighten the threshold for seizures, making it less likely that the person will have a fit. The downside of taking any sedative with K is that they tend to nullify one of its safety factors. K does not depress the respiratory system; sedatives do, and as the person nears the anesthetic state, using them in conjunction with K can result in an extremely dangerous situation. Sedatives also reduce many of the desired effects K-Heads seek, thus making the experience pretty much worthless.

The Handbook of Psychiatric Emergencies, on the other hand, recommends using a diazepam like Valium® as treatment for ketamine-induced disorders—presumably with a physician in attendance. Other substances researchers recommend avoiding while using K are antihistamines, such as Sudafed® and Tylenol Sinus® medicine, anti-nausea drugs, antibiotics, MDMA or ecstasy, GHB, Syrian Rue and yohimbine.

Chapter 9

Ketamine and the Law

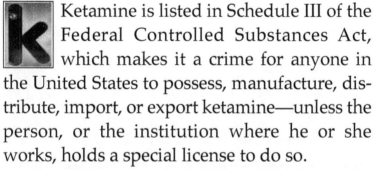 Ketamine is listed in Schedule III of the Federal Controlled Substances Act, which makes it a crime for anyone in the United States to possess, manufacture, distribute, import, or export ketamine—unless the person, or the institution where he or she works, holds a special license to do so.

Restrictions placed on ketamine and the mandatory minimum sentences associated with ketamine crimes are not as severe as for marijuana, cocaine, heroine, and many other drugs used recreationally. The reason is that drugs in Schedule III have accepted medical applications and are considered to have a reasonable safety level when used under medical supervision.

Federal Controlled Substances Act

To comprehend the meaning of ketamine's status as a Schedule III drug, you need some understanding of the Federal Controlled Substances Act as a whole. It was passed in 1970 and replaces all prior federal drug laws. Its purpose is to create a unified and consistent body of federal drug laws, which previously had been fragmentary and inconsistent. Despite some revisions and additions, the Federal Controlled Substances Act remains on the books in essentially the same form in which it originally appeared.

Drug Scheduling

The Federal Controlled Substances Act classifies drugs into five legal "Schedules." The tightest restrictions with severest penalties are associated with drugs placed in Schedule I. Restrictions and penalties progressively decrease for drugs placed in Schedules II through V.

Three factors determine the scheduling of a drug. These are: 1) the abuse potential of the drug; 2) whether or not the law considers the drug to have an acceptable level of safety when used under medical supervision; and 3) the presence or absence of medical uses for the drug that are accepted within the United States. When fresh data—which can include public opinion and other political factors—create a new consensus within the government regarding a particular substance, which is what happened with ketamine, a previously unscheduled drug can be added to the Act. Drugs can also be shifted from one Schedule to another.

Schedule I

Drugs placed in Schedule I are declared to have a high abuse potential with no currently accepted medical uses in the United States. Federal law considers these drugs to be unsafe even when used under medical supervision, which is prohibited.

Drugs in Schedule I include heroin, Acetylalphamethylfentanyl—a super-powerful synthetic opiate—and a number of other opiates and opiate derivatives. Several psychedelics—which federal law calls "hallucinogens"—such as psilocybin, peyote, DMT, and MDA also appear in Schedule I. The psychedelic LSD, popularly known as "acid," and MDMA, usually called "ecstasy," are listed in Schedule I despite the opinion of legions of psychiatrists and psychologists that these substances have significant therapeutic value. Marijuana is similarly a Schedule I drug despite its many widely accepted medical applications and wide-spread public opinion that it should be de-scheduled and legalized.

Schedule II

Drugs appearing in Schedule II have medical uses that are currently accepted within the United States and feature what federal lawmakers consider to be an acceptable level of safety when used under medical supervision. These drugs, however, are considered to have a high potential for abuse that can lead to severe psychological physical dependence.

Schedule II features a number of medically-used opiates such as morphine, administered widely in hospitals as a painkiller, and Methadone®, which is used as a form of substitution therapy for heroin and as a treatment for heroin withdrawal. Opium itself, the morphine-containing poppy-plant extract that is the mother of the all opiates and their derivatives, is a Schedule II drug as well. Additionally, mixtures containing sufficiently high quantities of codeine, which is an opiate, are placed in Schedule II.

The stimulants amphetamine and methamphetamine appear in Schedule II along with the opiates already mentioned. Schedule II also includes the one-time animal tranquilizer and wildly unpredictable hallucinogen PCP, popularly known as "angel dust." PCP is a close chemical cousin of ketamine, but its effects are much longer-lasting.

Schedule III

Drugs appearing in Schedule III have currently accepted medical uses in the United States and are considered by federal lawmakers to feature an acceptable level of safety when used under medical supervision. The abuse potential of Schedule III substances is evaluated to be lower than that of drugs in Schedules I and II. Abuse of Schedule III drugs is considered to hold the threat of low or moderate physical dependence but high psychological dependence.

Drugs placed in Schedule III include lysergic acid and lysergic acid amide. These natural substances can be used to manufacture LSD and have their own LSD-like effects. Also appearing in Schedule III are several anabolic steroids and some depressants. Federal law classifies ketamine in schedule III along with these substances.

Schedule IV

Drugs listed in Schedule IV have medical uses that are currently accepted in the United States and are considered to have lower abuse potential than drugs listed in Schedules I through III. Abuse of Schedule IV drugs is believed by lawmakers to hold the potential for less severe forms of physical and psychological dependence than is associated with substances in Schedules I through III.

Schedule IV features several barbiturates—which are heavy sedatives—including Phenobarbital®, the most well-known barbiturate. Schedule V also lists diazepam—commonly known as Valium®—and many other "minor tranquilizers" of the same general family, such as clonazepam. Phentermine® and Fenfluramine®, two popular and controversial appetite suppressants, are also included in Schedule IV.

Schedule V

Drugs placed in schedule V have currently accepted medical uses in the United States and are considered to have lower abuse and dependence potentials than the substances in Schedules I through IV. Schedule V drugs include Lumodil®, which is used to treat diarrhea, and Bupenorphine®, a substance used to treat heroin withdrawal. Mixtures containing relatively small concentrations of codeine—for instance, many cough formulas—also appear in Schedule V.

Ketamine's Legal History

Prior to 1990, there were few—if any—laws proscribing ketamine. As the 1990s progressed, however, a legal trend took place in which an increasing number of individual states passed their own laws against ketamine. This trend occurred largely in response to the burgeoning popularity of a nasally-ingested crystalline form of ketamine used at bars, nightclubs, and raves—and the medical incidents and negative publicity this spreading type of use generated.

Many of the states that passed these laws against ketamine have their own controlled substances acts that feature legal schedules closely parallel to those of the Federal Controlled Substances Act. As the state-by-state trend to outlaw ketamine progressed, states with drug laws structured according to the federal model generally placed ketamine in their version of Schedule III. California, Connecticut, Delaware, Florida, Georgia, Hawaii, Illinois, Indiana, Louisiana, Michigan, New Hampshire, New Jersey, New Mexico, Oklahoma, and Wisconsin all placed ketamine on Schedule III of their own controlled substances act or equivalent. Missouri and Tennessee, however, listed ketamine in their version of Schedule IV. The drug laws of Massachusetts, which feature a terminology somewhat different than that of the Federal Controlled Substances Act, listed ketamine as a "Class A" drug.

Prior to ketamine's placement in Federal Schedule III in 1999, unsuccessful efforts had already taken place to pass federal proscriptions against ketamine. The first attempt to assign ketamine to Federal Schedule III occurred all the way back in 1981. In 1996, Senator Joseph Biden, who described ketamine as an "incredibly popular drug," launched two campaigns to place the drug on Federal Schedule II. Finally, with the support of several veterinary associations and a recommendation from Health and Human Services, just a few months before the close of the millinium, the Drug Enforcement Administration placed ketamine in Schedule III.

Previously in 1996, legislation was passed which directed ketamine to be covered under the "Drug-Induced Rape Prevention and Punishment Act of 1996" which increased penalties for abuse of the drug.

The presence of this federal law does not obviate individual state laws against ketamine. In general, the defendant for a crime is tried and sentenced according to federal or state law depending on whether charges were originally brought by federal or state authorities.

Penalties

Accurately estimating the severity of the sentence that will be handed down under the Federal Controlled Substances Act for any given drug crime is difficult. In addition to the Schedule assigned to the drug involved, several other factors contribute to the formulation of sentences.

A major issue in sentencing is the amount of the drug involved: the higher the amount, the more severe the potential sentence. Exporting or trafficking an illegal drug, including possession of the drug with intent to commit these offenses, are crimes that bring down far more severe sentences than simple possession. Other factors that contribute to the severity of a sentence include the prior criminal history of the defendant, whether firearms or other weapons were present when the crime occurred, and whether the crime led to death or serious bodily injury.

The combination of these factors leads to forty-four different possible levels of sentencing for drug crimes under federal law. For crimes involving drugs in all five Schedules, potential federal sentences can range from no prison time at all to life imprisonment. The sentencing of drug crimes under individual state laws can be equally complex.

The Changing Nature of the Law

The law is always changing as new laws are put on the books and old ones are repealed. Furthermore, individual court cases are continually setting new precedents that redefine how laws are interpreted and applied. Keeping up with changes in the law and its interpretation by the courts can be accomplished only through ongoing and often complicated research. Drug law—including the legalities surrounding ketamine at any given time—offers no exception to these rules.

Basically, ketamine is against the law, including mere possession. Unless you can produce a doctor's perscription or have a medical license, you run the risk if getting busted if you are caught with it. With that said, we will close this book with an amusing anecdote about Timothy Leary relayed by Dan Joy.

The Leary Ketamine Bust

Among psychedelic pioneer Timothy Leary's many notorious encounters with the law, one of the most amusing—and least consequential—peripherally involved ketamine.

Back in the late 1970s, Leary's Los Angeles neighbors called the police because of disturbing noises emerging from the apartment he then shared with his new wife, Barbara.

The police arrived and took the Learys into custody. Meanwhile, they conducted a thorough search of the Leary's home, no doubt motivated by Timothy Leary's decades of much-publicized involvement with illegal drugs. The interview that the officers conducted with the Learys determined that the noises in question were the result of what the newspapers called "loud sex," and the search of the Leary home turned up no drugs other than a vial of ketamine (as usual, Leary was ahead of his time, experimenting with ketamine for its psychoactive effects years before this practice became popular). Since there were no laws against "loud sex" and since no serious legal proscriptions against non-medical use of ketamine existed at the time—

*in fact, the officers probably hadn't even heard
of the substance—the Learys were soon released from custody.*

*   *   *

EDITOR'S NOTE: Of course, we must suppose that
Timothy was "bullshitting", thereby mocking the press
since if he and Barbara had been on ketamine, it is
very unlikely that they would have been able to en-
gage in loud sex or make any noise at all!

Dr. Karl Jansen, MD, PhD

Dr. Karl Jansen is a psychiatrist with the South London and Maudsley NHS Trust and the Research Chief for JMS Research in London.

He has studied all aspects of ketamine, from where it binds in the human brain to its effects on popular culture, from addiction to ketamine's use as a treatment for addiction, from ketamine-induced near-birth to near-death experiences.

As part of his research Dr. Jansen is interviewing people about their experience using ketamine for recreational and spiritual purposes.

To contact Dr. Jansen
email him at K@BTInternet.com
Or write to 13 Ann Moss Way
London SE16 2TH, UK.

THE RESONANCE PROJECT

THE JOURNAL OF MODERN PSYCHEDELIC CULTURE

The Resonance Project (TRP) is a mainstream print periodical dedicated to the study of psychedelics, expanded consciousness, and the science of reality and perception. The goal of TRP is to provide a public forum for the discussion of entheogens, to investigate modern psychedelic trends and culture, and to dissemenate accurate information about entheogens. TRP is published by Resonant Media, a privately funded not-for-profit business.

TRP is published twice a year, usually in the winter and summer. TRP is available by subscription and is sold on newsstands nationwide. If you would like to buy a specific issue of TRP, you can order single issues online directly from Resonant Media.

TRP is always looking for quality writing and artwork for publication. If you are a writer or an artist and you would like to contribute something, please take a look at our Submission Guidelines. If you have other skills that you would like to contribute to TRP, please see our Volunteer Page for more information on what kinds of help we're looking for.

Resonant Media
323 Broadway Ave. E. #318
Seattle, WA 981092
voice mail: 206-587-7177
e-mail: trp@resproject.com

www.resproject.com

THE VAULTS OF EROWID

PLANTS & DRUGS   MIND & SPIRIT   FREEDOM & LAW   ARTS & SCIENCES

A free online library of information about psychoactive chemicals and plants, medicinal herbs, pharmaceuticals and nootropics, focusing on healthy, responsible, beneficial use. Erowid has collected thousands of pages of up-to-date information since 1996 to help people learn about the complex relationship between humans and psychoactive drugs.

All the Basics
Effects • Dosages • Methods • Durations • Personal Experience Reports • FAQs • Drug Testing Info • Thousands of Organized Links

Safety Information
Common Problems • Contraindications • Drug Interactions • Health Concerns • Addiction Potentials • Idiosyncratic Reactions

Images
Over 800 well organized photos and drawings of psychoactive plants, chemicals, and herbs from around the world.

Law
State and Federal Legal Info • Text of Controlled Substance Laws

Spiritual & Cultural Use
Ethnobotany • Ethnopharmacology • Traditional, Spiritual, Medicinal Use • Modern Cultural Use

Chemistry
Chemicals Names • Chemical Formulas • Molecular Structures

Resources
Medical Research • Studies • Summaries • Reviews • Abstracts Government Reports • Cultivation Tips • Vendor Lists

Literature
Media and News Reports • Short-Stories • Online Books • Library and Bookstore • Bibliographies

www.erowid.org

THE LYCÆUM

The World's largest entheogenic library and community

The Lycaeum is an online service a little different from others. The single focus of this server is visionary plants and chemicals. All of the Lycaeum online services revolve around the goal of distributing information about visionary plants and chemicals to an established home-spun community.

The Lycæum was born from the Visionary Plants List (VPL), a now-retired Internet mailing list that was subscribed to by many people with a common interest in the entheogenic experience. We officially opened our doors on June 22, 1996, as a place where people from all around the world could freely exchange and research information regarding visionary plants, fungi, and chemicals. Since that time, we have had millions of visitors and have grown to become one of the Internet's largest hubs of drug information.

The Lycaeum is built with community strongly in mind. The online forums and conferences provide social interaction that allows the member to meet like-minded people from all over the world. We strongly support the free exchange of information. We regard our plant, fungal, and chemical teachers with the utmost respect.

The Lycaeum puts out an incredible human effort to help facilitate the publishing of novel information. In turn, we release this information for free to the world at large. We try our best to make sure that information is accurate as can be.

THE LYCÆUM

www.lycaeum.org